Mountain Gorillas
in Danger

by Helen Orme

ticktock

CONTENTS

Words that appear **in bold** are explained in the glossary.

Copyright © **ticktock Entertainment Ltd** 2008
First published in Great Britain in 2008 by **ticktock Media Ltd**,
Unit 2, Orchard Business Centre, North Farm Road,
Tunbridge Wells, Kent, TN2 3XF
ISBN 978 1 84696 779 5 pbk
Printed in China

We would like to thank Penny Worms, the National Literacy Trust, and our consultant Dr. Annette Lanjouw,
Director of the International Gorilla Conservation Programme

Picture credits: t=top, b=bottom, c=centre, l-left, r=right
Corbis: 15. Digital Vision: 4-5, 6-7, 8-9, 10-11, 12-13, 14, 18-19b, 22-23, 24-25, 26-27,
28-29, 30-31, 32. FLPA: OFC, 20-21. Nature Picture Library: 16-17, 18-19t,
Every effort has been made to trace the copyright holders, and we apologise in advance for any unintentional omissions. We would
be pleased to insert the appropriate acknowledgements in any subsequent edition of this publication.

A VERY RARE ANIMAL

Mountain gorillas are one of the rarest animals in the world.

There are only about 720 mountain gorillas and they live in just two places in Africa. Both places are in **protected parks**, high up in the mountains.

The gorillas live in thick, misty **rainforests** on the mountain slopes. Some of the mountains are **dormant volcanoes**.

These are the Virunga volcanoes in Rwanda. Half the mountain gorillas live here.

WHERE THEY LIVE

AFRICA

UGANDA

THE DEMOCRATIC REPUBLIC OF CONGO

RWANDA

The protected parks are shown in green on this map.

YOUNG MOUNTAIN GORILLAS

A baby gorilla weighs about two kilograms when it is born.

For the first few months, the mother gorilla will hold the baby to her chest. As it gets older, the mother will carry the baby on her back.

When gorillas are about a year old they will climb trees and play on their own, but they never stray far from their family group.

GORILLA FAMILIES

A gorilla family will have one or two adult male gorillas, some adult females, and some babies and young gorillas.

Some adult male gorillas are called silverbacks. This is because they have silvery fur growing on their back and hips.

Each gorilla family has a silverback as leader. The silverback protects the group.

SILVERBACK FACT

Silverbacks keep other animals away from their families by acting tough! They stand on their back legs and beat their chests.

LOOKING FOR FOOD

*Gorillas spend their day moving through the forest **foraging** for food. An adult gorilla can eat up to 30 kilograms of food every day.*

Mountain gorillas are mainly plant eaters. They eat stinging nettles, bamboo, thistles, berries and other leafy plants.

Sometimes they will eat worms, grubs and ants.

BABY FOOD FACT

Baby gorillas drink their mothers' milk until they are about two years old.

Gorillas have strong jaws and large teeth for grinding up tough plant stalks. They get almost all the water they need from eating plants.

DIFFICULT TIMES FOR MOUNTAIN GORILLAS

Mountain gorillas were discovered by non-African people 100 years ago. Many hunters came to Africa to kill them.

At last people realised that there were fewer and fewer gorillas.

Many zoos were able to protect the lowland gorillas. Mountain gorillas could not be protected in this way because they died when they were kept in a zoo.

The areas where the gorillas live became protected parks and hunting them was against the law.

MORE DANGERS

Things slowly began to get better for mountain gorillas, but in 1990 a terrible war broke out in this part of Africa.

People hid in the mountains. Some gorillas caught diseases from the people.

One of the dangers today is that many people live near the protected parks. These people need land for farming and wood for fuel. This destroys the gorillas' **habitat**. Helping the people who live near gorillas is as important as helping the gorillas themselves.

People cut down trees for firewood.

POACHERS

Poaching is another problem for the mountain gorillas.

Usually poachers are not trying to catch gorillas. The poachers are hunting for antelopes or bush pigs, which they can take home to eat. The poachers use **snares** to catch these animals.

Sometimes gorillas get caught in these snares.

In this picture, **park rangers** are carrying the body of an adult gorilla that died when it was caught in a poacher's snare.

PEOPLE WHO HELP

Life is difficult for the mountain gorillas, but there are people whose job it is to help them.

Park rangers patrol the forest. They help any gorilla who is ill or in trouble.

The mountain gorillas have their own special vets. The vets can go into the forest to treat the gorillas.

In this picture, the rangers are checking on a gorilla who is ill. The silverback is trying to guard his family.

GORILLA TOURISTS

It might seem a bad thing for **tourists** *to visit the mountain gorillas. However, if the number of tourists is controlled, it can help them.*

Gorilla tourists bring money and jobs to this part of Africa. This makes it even more important for local people to protect the gorillas.

The tourists are only allowed to stay with the animals for an hour. They cannot go closer than seven metres.

This keeps the mountain gorillas safe from human diseases.

GENTLE GIANTS

People often think gorillas are fierce. In fact, they are gentle, intelligent animals.

HELPING THE MOUNTAIN GORILLAS

Mountain gorillas have survived hunting, war and disease.

Their numbers are beginning to go up slowly.

Now local people are earning money from tourists who come to see the gorillas, they want to protect the gorillas and the forest.

This is not just a good thing for the gorillas. It helps *all* the plants and animals that live in the forest.

GLOSSARY

apes A group of mammals that includes gorillas, chimpanzees, orang-utans and humans.

dormant volcanoes Volcanoes that haven't erupted for a long time, but might erupt again in the future.

foraging Looking for food in the wild.

habitat The place that suits a particular wild animal or plant.

park rangers People whose job is to look after protected parks and the animals that live there.

protected parks Areas where hunting animals or cutting down trees is against the law.

rainforest Warm, wet forests, often found near the Equator, where there are many types of plants and animals.

snares Traps made from a loop of wire. When an animal treads on the wire, it springs up and holds the animal's leg. The more the animal struggles, the tighter the wire becomes.

tourists People who are on holiday.

INDEX